Unsheltered
Barbara Kingsolver

Conversation Starters

By Paul Adams
Book Habits

Please Note: This is an unofficial Conversation Starters guide. If you have not yet read the original work, you can purchase the original book here.

Copyright © 2018 by BookHabits. All Rights Reserved. First Published in the United States of America 2018

We hope you enjoy this complimentary guide from BookHabits. Our mission is to aid readers and reading groups with quality thought-provoking material to in the discovery and discussions on some of today's favorite books.

Disclaimer / Terms of Use: This guide is unofficial and unauthorized. It is not authorized, approved, licensed, or endorsed by the original book's author or publisher and any of their licensees or affiliates. Product names, logos, brands, and other trademarks featured or referred to within this publication are the property of their respective trademark holders and are not affiliated with BookHabits. The publisher and author make no representations or warranties with respect to the accuracy or completeness of these contents and disclaim all warranties such as warranties of fitness for a particular purpose.
No part of this publication may be reproduced or retransmitted, electronic or mechanical, without the written permission of the publisher.

Bonus Downloads
*Get Free Books with **Any Purchase** of Conversation Starters!*

Every purchase comes with a FREE download!

Add spice to any conversation
Never run out of things to say
Spend time with those you love

Get it Now

or Click Here.

Scan Your Phone

Tips for Using Conversation Starters:

EVERY GOOD BOOK CONTAINS A WORLD FAR DEEPER THAN the surface of its pages. Questions herein are designed to bring us beneath the surface of the page and invite us into the world that lives on. These questions can be used to:

- Foster a deeper understanding of the book
- Promote an atmosphere of discussion for groups
- Assist in the study of the book, either individually or corporately
- Explore unseen realms of the book as never seen before

Table of Contents

Introducing *Unsheltered* 6
Discussion Questions 15
Introducing the Author 36
Fireside Questions... 44
Quiz Questions 55
Quiz Answers... 68
Ways to Continue Your Reading 69

Introducing *Unsheltered*

Unsheltered: A Novel is written by American author Barbara Kingsolver. It is a portrait of lives lived in two different periods in American history and yet so similar in the social and political challenges that defined them. It tells the stories of two families who live in the same house but in two different eras. Willa lives in an old house in Vineland, New Jersey. A freelance journalist who feels increasingly hard keeping up with the economically challenging times, she learns that her house needs a major repair. Its foundation needs restoration. She does her research and finds out that the house once belonged to Thatcher Greenwood, a man who lived in the 1870s. Greenwood is a science teacher who, like Willa, is caught in difficult circumstances during his time. He is excited by Charles Darwin's recently published work but is forbidden to talk about it. He suspects his house is not safe and sturdy, but his wife and in-laws don't want to know about it because it will cause an embarrassing scandal. He befriends a woman scientist who puts him in conflict with the powerful men in town. Meanwhile, Willa, living in contemporary times, faces a family tragedy that renders her grandchild motherless. She and her husband have worked so hard all these years and yet their family and their old house are falling apart.

The novel is structured using two narratives occurring in the past and the present. Two sets of characters live in the same house in Vineland, New Jersey. One family lives in the house during the post- Civil War while the other family lives in the modern age. The author says she used this literary device in order to help her understand the cultural crisis we live in today, by looking back at the past. It involves using a historical lens. Kingsolver compares the scientific attitudes prevalent during the Victorian period and today's Trump era. The Victorians had to confront the implications of Darwin's evolution theory with respect to the Judeo-Christian beliefs about creation. Darwin's theory caused some shocking realizations during that time and many were not prepared to discard old beliefs. In the same way today, people have to confront the scientific reality of global warming. Kingsolver's novel reflects her impassioned and critical thoughts about today's politicians who don't care about science and the future of civilization. The author tackles the question - "How do people behave in moments of cultural crisis?" It shows that when people are afraid, they look for protection from some leader who promises them some assurances. Kingsolver says the book is about "how desperately we hold on to our old worldviews, even when they no longer serve us, and how we overlook a lot of things to find reassurance."

The novel's theme includes the nature and effects of globalization and the failure of the American dream. In researching for the character of Mary Treat, Kingsolver discovered a lot of materials kept by the Historical Society. Mary Treat was a real person who lived in the 1870s in Vineland. She corresponded with Darwin and their letters were used by Kingsolver as part of her research. She says many of the things Treat says in the novel were her actual words taken from her own writings. Willa's character is at the center of the novel. It shows her taking on the stress caused by the difficulties experienced by the younger generations. She had expectations that as she and her husband grow older, life will get easier because they have prepared the younger generation to responsibly manage their lives. But external social circumstances changed and life for them became even harder. At the root of Willa's unhappiness and dissatisfaction is her failure to see that things are not the same anymore, and her expectations are not met. The title of the book alludes to the feeling of being unsheltered when one finds oneself unmoored from old beliefs and patterns, including beliefs about how the world functions. She uses the metaphor of a crumbling old house to highlight the uncertainty of shifting foundations that threaten families and nations into falling down. Critics applaud the author's humor even as she tackles serious sociopolitical issues.

The Washington Post review says the characters of Willa and Thatcher echo each other in "curious and provocative ways, though set apart by 140 years. The review cites the author's message of the difficult experience of being unsheltered, " cast out from the comforts of old beliefs about how the world works..." The *San Francisco Chronicle* says the author has "truly believable characters" who find themselves in "hardscrabble circumstances..." This makes the book captivating and thought-provoking. *O, the Oprah Magazine* review says the novel makes readers weep but it is also hilarious. It shows how people "navigate profound changes that threaten to unmoor us." T*he Guardian* review says the book is "a powerful lament for the American dream..." It is, accordingly, a powerful evocation of the eerie experience of living in socially uncertain times. The review cites the author's supreme craftsmanship and ingenious metaphors. At the heart of her narratives are social questions. The *Boston Globe* review says the novel points to a doubtful future as far the world is concerned. The author's voice is eloquent and urgent, "laced with wry, genial humor." The novel is also a stark narrative of "how battling schools of thought can destroy personal lives."

Unsheltered is authored by Kingsolver whose novels are known for tackling social and political issues. Her 1998 novel, *The Poisonwood Bible*, is a

Pulitzer Prize finalist. Her other books include *Flight Behavior*; and *Animal, Vegetable, Miracle*.

Discussion Questions

"Get Ready to Enter a New World"

Tip: Begin with questions dealing with broader issues to ensure ample time for quality discussions. Read through all discussion questions before engaging.

~~~

question 1

Willa lives in an old house in Vineland, New Jersey. A freelance journalist who feels increasingly hard keeping up with the economically challenging times, she learns that her house needs a major repair. How does she react when she is told that her house no foundation at all?

~~~

~~~

question 2

She does her research and finds out that the house once belonged to Thatcher Greenwood, a man who lived in the 1870s. Greenwood is a science teacher who, like Willa, is caught in difficult circumstances during his time. How does Willa feel about Thatcher? What does she think about him living in a house without a foundation?

~~~

~~~

question 3

Thatcher is excited by Charles Darwin's recently published work but is forbidden to talk about it. Why? What is at stake if Darwin's ideas become popular?

~~~

~~~

question 4

Willa faces a family tragedy that renders her grandchild motherless. She and her husband have worked so hard all these years and yet their family and their old house are falling apart. How does she feel about her circumstances? Who does she blame?

~~~

~ ~ ~

question 5

Two sets of characters live in the same house in Vineland, New Jersey. One family lives in the house during the post- Civil War while the other family lives in the modern age. What effect does the author create in putting two families in one house at two different eras? How do you feel reading about them?

~ ~ ~

question 6

The novel is structured using two narratives occurring in the past and the present. How does the author transition from one time period to another? Do you find the two narratives easy to follow? Do you find it confusing?

~~~

question 7

The author says she used this literary device in order to help her understand the cultural crisis we live in today, by looking back at the past. It involves using a historical lens. Do you think it is an effective device? Are you able to have a better understanding of today's problems by looking at the past? Why? Why not?

~~~

question 8

Kingsolver compares the scientific attitudes prevalent during the Victorian period and today's Trump era. The Victorians had to confront the implications of Darwin's evolution theory with respect to the Judeo-Christian beliefs about creation. How did the Victorians regard Darwin's theory? Do you find similarity in today's scientific discoveries about global warming? What similarities in people's reactions do you find?

~ ~ ~

question 9

Darwin's theory caused some shocking realizations during that time and many were not prepared to discard old beliefs. In the same way today, people have to confront the scientific reality of global warming. Does the novel enlighten you about your attitudes toward global warming? Do you think you need to change your attitude toward it?

~ ~ ~

~ ~ ~

question 10

Kingsolver's novel reflects her impassioned and critical thoughts about today's politicians who don't care about science and the future of civilization. How does she portray politicians in the novel? What attitudes do they have that the author criticizes?

~ ~ ~

~~~

question 11

The novel's theme includes the nature and effects of globalization and the failure of the American dream. How does she tackle the theme of the American dream? Which characters embody this theme? In what way?

~~~

question 12

In researching for the character of Mary Treat, Kingsolver discovered a lot of materials kept by the Historical Society. Mary Treat was a real person who lived in the 1870s in Vineland. She corresponded with Darwin and their letters were used by Kingsolver as part of her research. She says many of the things she says in the novel were her actual words taken from her own writings. How does her research help her in bringing the character to life? Which factual information does she use to illustrate her character?

~~~

question 13

Willa's character is at the center of the novel. It shows her taking on the stress caused by the difficulties experienced by the younger generations. She had expectations that as she and her husband grow older, life will get easier because they have prepared the younger generation to responsibly manage their lives. What happens to her expectations?

~~~

~~~

question 14

The title of the book alludes to the feeling of being unsheltered when one finds oneself unmoored from old beliefs and patterns, including beliefs about how the world functions.
She uses the metaphor of a crumbling old house to highlight the uncertainty of shifting foundations that threaten families and nations into falling down. Do you think it's a good title? Why? Why not?

~~~

~ ~ ~

question 15

Critics applaud the author's humor even as she tackles serious sociopolitical issues. Which passages do you find funny? How does the humor affect the book's serious themes?

~ ~ ~

~~~

question 16

The Washington Post review says the characters of Willa and Thatcher echo each other in "curious and provocative ways, though set apart by 140 years. How do the two characters echo each other?

~~~

~~~

question 17

The San Francisco Chronicle says the author has "truly believable characters" who find themselves in "hardscrabble circumstances..." This makes the book captivating and thought-provoking. How does the author make them believable?

~~~

~~~

question 18

O, the Oprah Magazine review says the novel makes readers weep but it is also hilarious. It shows how people "navigate profound changes that threaten to unmoor us." Which parts in the novel made you weep? Why?

~~~

~~~

question 19

The Guardian review says the book is "a powerful lament for the American dream..." It is, accordingly, a powerful evocation of the eerie experience of living in socially uncertain times. The review cites the author's supreme craftsmanship and ingenious metaphors. At the heart of her narratives are social questions. What examples in the novel can you cite as characteristic of supreme craftsmanship? Which are examples of ingenious metaphors?

~~~

~~~

question 20

The Boston Globe review says the novel points to a doubtful future as far the world is concerned. The author's voice is eloquent and urgent, "laced with wry, genial humor." The novel is also a stark narrative of "how battling schools of thought can destroy personal lives." Whose lives were destroyed as a result of warring schools of thought? How were they destroyed?

~~~

Introducing the Author

Barbara Kingsolver is known to start her novels by asking questions. In thinking about *Unsheltered*, she had been asking the question "what the heck is going on?" She had noticed that recent national and world events do not follow the well-worn rules anymore. Social, political, biological, and environmental rules have been changing in the past years. Three years ago, when she started writing the book, she realized that she needed to write a book about "how people behave in moments of cultural crisis." She is excited to release her most recent work because it has asked questions that involve the political and social turmoil that affect Americans today. She says the novel is supposed to ask questions, not propose answers. She hopes readers will ask themselves these questions and to have conversations as a result.

In asking herself the question, Kingsolver thinks that people tend to let their fears take hold of them in times of cultural crisis. People look for leaders who will reassure them, "even if those leaders behave like tyrannical bullies." She says her book shows how people are desperate in holding on to their old views even if these do not work anymore. A lot of things are overlooked in their desire to be reassured. In order to understand the current cultural crisis, she chose to use look into history.

The 1870s were a period of cultural crisis when Charles Darwin's theory about evolution made people question their existential origins. Darwin and the other scientists of that time were coming to the conclusion that humans are part of the natural world. This idea was so threatening to the people in that century. The real-life character of Mary Treat is someone Kingsolver can relate with. Kingsolver is a trained biologist, just like Mary Treat. Very little was known about her but in the course of her research, Kingsolver found that the woman scientist had done a lot of scientific work and that she corresponded with Charles Darwin. Kingsolver was thrilled about her and her discovery.

Kingsolver has written critically acclaimed fiction and non-fiction books since she started writing in 1985. Her first novel, *The Bean Trees*, came out in 1988. This was followed by *Homeland* (1989), *Holding the Line: Women in the Great Arizona Mine Strike* (1989), *Animal Dreams* (1990), and many more. In 1998, she published *The Poisonwood Bible* which won South Africa's national book award and was named a finalist for the Orange Prize and the Pulitzer Prize. Many of her books are taught in high schools and colleges throughout the country. She won the National Humanities Medal in 2000 and is Writers Digest's one of the most important writers of the 20th century. *Animal, Vegetable, Miracle* won her the James Beard award, among other awards. Her *The Lacuna* won the Orange Prize for Fiction. She supports aspiring writers through her Bellwether Prize for Fiction which awards unpublished first novels. The award is now known as the PEN/Bellwether Prize for Socially Engaged Fiction.

Apart from reading material for her research, she says she constantly reads fiction. "My rule is that I read fiction that is so good, I wish I could have written it myself," she says. She also reads poetry, "like the last thing at night. It cleans up your brain, makes it better, fills it with really beautiful words."

Kingsolver reveals that she kept a journal when she was eight years old. The journal was colored red and it came with a lock. It encouraged her to write every day. When her school teachers assigned her class some writing exercises, she always wrote so many extra pages than the required, "a surfeit of juvenile prose I am sure they came to dread," she says. She joined all essay writing contests in her school. Her very first published work was entitled "Why We Need a New Elementary School." It tells the exciting story of how her school ceiling fell and hurt her teacher. The essay was published in the local newspaper.

Kingsolver earned her master's degree in biology from the University of Arizona. She did not, however, finish her dissertation because she took a writing job at the university. She realized that if she kept on writing, she can earn enough to pay the rent.

She started writing for newspapers, covering the science beat and eventually writing about the arts and investigative journalism. She decided to quit her full-time job at the university in 1985 and do freelance writing which was her passion. She says she never looked back after that.

Bonus Downloads
*Get Free Books with **Any Purchase** of Conversation Starters!*

Every purchase comes with a FREE download!

Add spice to any conversation
Never run out of things to say
Spend time with those you love

Get it Now

or Click Here.

Scan Your Phone

Fireside Questions

"What would you do?"

Tip: These questions can be a fun exercise as it spurs creativity among the readers by allowing alternate scene endings and "if this was you" questions.

~~~

question 21

Three years ago, when she started writing the book, she realized that she needed to write a book about "how people behave in moments of cultural crisis." She is excited to release her most recent work because it has asked questions that involve the political and social turmoil that affect Americans today. She says the novel is supposed to ask questions, not propose answers. What questions were asked in the novel? Have you asked yourself questions as a result of reading the novel? What were these?

~~~

~~~

question 22

The real-life character of Mary Treat is someone Kingsolver can relate with. Kingsolver is a trained biologist, just like Mary Treat. Very little was known about her but in the course of her research, Kingsolver found that the woman scientist had done a lot of scientific work and that she corresponded with Charles Darwin. Kingsolver was thrilled about her and her discovery. What have you learned about Mary Treat through the novel?

~~~

question 23

Kingsolver has written critically acclaimed fiction and non-fiction books since she started writing in 1985. Her first novel, The Bean Trees, came out in 1988. This was followed by Homeland (1989), Holding the Line: Women in the Great Arizona Mine Strike (1989), Animal Dreams (1990), and many more. Which of her other books have you read? What are the themes in her books?

~~~

question 24

She supports aspiring writers through her Bellwether Prize for Fiction which awards unpublished first novels. The award is now known as the PEN/Bellwether Prize for Socially Engaged Fiction. Why do you think she needs to support aspiring writers?

~~~

~~~

question 25

In 1998, she published The Poisonwood Bible which won South Africa's national book award and was named a finalist for the Orange Prize and the Pulitzer Prize. Have you read the book? Why do you think it is critically acclaimed?

~~~

question 26

The novel is structured using two narratives occurring in the past and the present. Two sets of characters live in the same house in Vineland, New Jersey. One family lives in the house during the post- Civil War while the other family lives in the modern age. The author says she used this literary device in order to help her understand the cultural crisis we live in today, by looking back at the past. It involves using a historical lens. Kingsolver compares the scientific attitudes prevalent during the Victorian period and today's Trump era. If you are to choose a different period in the past that would similarly compare with present-day cultural and political issues, what period would it be? Why?

~~~

~~~

question 27

In researching for the character of Mary Treat, Kingsolver discovered a lot of materials kept by the Historical Society. Mary Treat was a real person who lived in the 1870s in Vineland. She corresponded with Darwin and their letters were used by Kingsolver as part of her research. She says many of the things she says in the novel were her actual words taken from her own writings. If you are to write about an unknown real-life character from the past, who would it be? Why?

~~~

~~~

question 28

Willa's character is at the center of the novel. It shows her taking on the stress caused by the difficulties experienced by the younger generations. She had expectations that as she and her husband grow older, life will get easier because they have prepared the younger generation to responsibly manage their lives. But external social circumstances changed and life for them became even harder. At the root of Willa's unhappiness and dissatisfaction is her failure to see that things are not the same anymore, and her expectations are not met. If Willa is a man, how will it change the story? What actions would he take that Willa does not?

~~~

question 29

The 1870s were a period of cultural crisis when Charles Darwin's theory about evolution made people question their existential origins. Darwin and the other scientists of that time were coming to the conclusion that humans are part of the natural world. This idea was so threatening to the people in that century. If the Judeo-Christian belief about creation prevailed over Darwin's theory at that time, how different would the world be today?

~ ~ ~

question 30

The title of the book alludes to the feeling of being unsheltered when one finds oneself unmoored from old beliefs and patterns, including beliefs about how the world functions. She uses the metaphor of a crumbling old house to highlight the uncertainty of shifting foundations that threaten families and nations into falling down. If you are to suggest another title for this novel, what would it be? Why?

~ ~ ~

Quiz Questions

"Ready to Announce the Winners?"

Tip: Create a leaderboard and track scores to see who gets the most correct answers. Winners required. Prizes optional.

~~~

quiz question 1

Two sets of characters live in the same house in _____. One family lives in the house during the post- Civil War while the other family lives in the modern age.

~~~

~~~

quiz question 2

_____is a science teacher who, like Willa, is caught in difficult circumstances during his time. He is excited by Charles Darwin's recently published work but is forbidden to talk about it.

~~~

~~~

quiz question 3

_____ was a real person who lived in the 1870s in Vineland. She corresponded with Darwin and their letters were used by Kingsolver as part of her research. She says many of the things Treat says in the novel were her actual words taken from her own writings.

~~~

~~~

quiz question 4

True or False: Willa's character is at the center of the novel. It shows her taking on the stress caused by the difficulties experienced by the younger generations.

~~~

~~~

quiz question 5

True or False: The title of the book alludes to the feeling of being unsheltered when one finds oneself unmoored from old beliefs and patterns.

~~~

~~~

quiz question 6

True or False: She uses the metaphor of a bombed high-rise building to highlight the uncertainty of shifting foundations that threaten families and nations into falling down.

~~~

~~~

quiz question 7

True or False: Critics applaud the author's humor even as she tackles serious sociopolitical issues.

~~~

~~~

quiz question 8

In 1998, she published _____ which won South Africa's national book award and was named a finalist for the Orange Prize and the Pulitzer Prize.

~~~

~~~

quiz question 9

Her book _____ won the Orange Prize for Fiction.

~~~

~~~

quiz question 10

She supports aspiring writers through her Bellwether Prize for Fiction which awards unpublished first novels. The award is now known as the PEN/Bellwether Prize for Socially Engaged Fiction.

~~~

~~~

quiz question 11

True or False: She says her book shows how people are desperate in holding on to their old views even if these do not work anymore.

~~~

~~~

quiz question 12

True or False: She won the Nobel Prize in 2000.

~~~

Quiz Answers

1. Vineland, New Jersey
2. Thatcher Greenwood
3. Mary Treat
4. True
5. True
6. False
7. True
8. The Poisonwood Bible
9. The Lacuna
10. True
11. True
12. False

Ways to Continue Your Reading

EVERY month, our team runs through a wide selection of books to pick the best titles for readers and reading groups, and promotes these titles to our thousands of readers – sometimes with free downloads, sale dates, and additional brochures.

Click here to sign up for these benefits.

If you have not yet read the original work or would like to read it again, you can purchase the original book here.

Bonus Downloads
*Get Free Books with **Any Purchase** of* Conversation Starters!

Every purchase comes with a FREE download!

Add spice to any conversation
Never run out of things to say
Spend time with those you love

Get it Now

or Click Here.

Scan Your Phone

On the Next Page…

If you found this book helpful to your discussions and rate it a 4 or 5, please write us a review on the next page.

Any length would be fine but we'd appreciate hearing you more! We'd be very encouraged.

Till next time,

BookHabits

"Loving Books is Actually a Habit"

CPSIA information can be obtained
at www.ICGtesting.com
Printed in the USA
BVHW030245310520
580411BV00003B/436